W9-CFK-772

Makerspace Careers

CAREERS IN

ROBOTICS

CAROL HAND

Rosen
YA

New York

Published in 2020 by The Rosen Publishing Group, Inc.
29 East 21st Street, New York, NY 10010

Library of Congress Cataloging-in-Publication Data

Names: Hand, Carol, 1945– author.
Title: Careers in robotics / Carol Hand.
Description: First edition. | New York : Rosen Publishing, 2020 |
Series: Makerspace careers | Audience: Grades 7–12. | Includes
bibliographical references and index.
Identifiers: LCCN 2018048168| ISBN 9781508188131 (library
bound) | ISBN 9781508188124 (paperback)
Subjects: LCSH: Robotics—Vocational guidance.
Classification: LCC TJ211.25 .H36 2020 | DDC 629.8/92023—dc23
LC record available at https://lccn.loc.gov/2018048168

Manufactured in China

CONTENTS

INTRODUCTION 4

CHAPTER ONE
FINDING AND WORKING IN MAKERSPACES 7

CHAPTER TWO
FROM MAKERSPACES TO ROBOTICS CAREERS 17

CHAPTER THREE
HOME AND MEDICAL ROBOTICS CAREERS 27

CHAPTER FOUR
INDUSTRIAL AND MILITARY ROBOTICS CAREERS 37

CHAPTER FIVE
PREPARING FOR A ROBOTICS CAREER 47

CHAPTER SIX
FINDING A JOB IN ROBOTICS 57

GLOSSARY 67
FOR MORE INFORMATION 70
FOR FURTHER READING 73
BIBLIOGRAPHY 74
INDEX... 77

INTRODUCTION

Excellent education has always involved giving students the chance to do things themselves, to learn by creating, making, and practicing. In the past, these opportunities have often been haphazard, done only when time, space, and materials permit. But modern educators are accepting the challenge of educating students for the technological future. They are implementing STEM programs, which provide interdisciplinary education in the areas of science, technology, engineering, and math, or STEAM programs, which add the arts. Educators are integrating applied design, skills, and technologies into school programs. Often, they do this by designing student makerspaces.

What is a makerspace? One of the best definitions comes from Michelle Davis, winner of the Canadian Innovators in Education Award in 2015–2016. In an article by A. Campbell, Davis says, "A Makerspace is a place that enables 'student making'; it inspires creation, invites problem-solving, risk-taking, collaboration and experimentation; it encourages our students to identify as 'creators of content,' rather than mere consumers of it." In short, a makerspace is a special place designed for students to work on exciting real-world problems that channel their creative impulses and build their skills.

At Gleneagles, an elementary school in West Vancouver, British Columbia, Canada, the makerspace is run by

The learning by doing that happens in a makerspace stimulates both creativity and skill development. Here, students in a makerspace develop measurement skills while cutting wood for a project.

Davis, Charity Cantlie, and Cari Wilson. It introduces young students to robotics through six fun makerspace stations. At Station 1, students use iPads to program two Spheros (tennis-ball-sized robots). They can program the Spheros to roll in any direction, spin, flip, and change colors. At Station 2, they work with the VEX Robotic Station, where they can create functional robots using LEGO-like kits that snap together. At Station 3, students build their own robots using simple materials such as cardboard, cups, and tape. Station 4 promotes literacy. Students are asked to create their own online robot-related story using Storybird, an iPad app. At Station 5, they work with motorized, programmable cubes called Cubelets, which snap together and stay connected by means of magnetic faces. Cubelets can be combined in many ways to form exciting new inventions. Finally, at Station 6, students learn science fiction writer Isaac Asimov's laws of robotics and the history and invention of these laws.

Makerspaces can begin in elementary schools such as Gleneagles. Projects become increasingly advanced in high school and college. According to a 2017 study by the New Media Consortium and the Consortium for School Networking, coding and robotics makerspaces will be trending topics in schools over the next five years. The emphasis on coding is based on the understanding that computer literacy will be as important for future students as reading and writing. As high school and college students build and program robots of increasing complexity, many of them will participate in robotics competitions. These competitions will help them tackle specific, real-world challenges—and give them a leg up into future robotics careers.

CHAPTER ONE

FINDING AND WORKING IN MAKERSPACES

Makerspaces are playgrounds for learning about twenty-first-century technologies, such as robotics. They are one of the best ways to develop knowledge and skills and to prepare for exciting careers in these up-and-coming fields. But not every school has a makerspace. How do you find or recognize a makerspace? Or, if there is no makerspace in your school, how do you make one? Once you have a makerspace, how exactly is it used?

FINDING OR FORMING MAKERSPACES

Makerspaces vary, depending on the school or the location outside the school. They are each unique because they are designed by individuals. A makerspace does not have to be a dedicated room. It may be located in a corner of the school library or media center. It can encompass the

Members of a robotics team in Wellsville, New York, make adjustments to the electrical system of their robot. Real-world problem solving is one important goal of a makerspace.

classroom or areas within the classroom. Spaces and materials will differ, depending on the project. Teachers might turn their classroom into a makerspace for a short time, once or several times a year, to do specific projects. They might set up stations around the room and have students rotate through them, making something different but related at each station. They might set up a makerspace cart that can move between classrooms, with materials changing with the project.

MAKERSPACE OR HACKERSPACE?

Some people define makerspaces by the presence of technological equipment, such as 3D printers, laser cutters, CNC (computer numerical control) machines, and robots. These are definitely a part of many makerspaces, but they are not essential. According to the website Makerspaces.com, the tools matter much less than the mind-set. A maker mind-set is more about "creating something out of nothing and exploring your own interests," the website says. The idea of makerspaces comes from the 1990s, when the first hackerspaces were formed. These were places where groups of computer programmers worked together to "hack" programs, taking them apart, learning about them, and revising them to do new tasks. Later, as fabrication tools such as 3D printers and laser cutters became affordable, hackerspaces evolved into makerspaces. Today, because the term "hacker" has developed a negative connotation, most people now prefer the term "makerspace."

A makerspace may simply be the science lab, where students engage in creative, exploratory work rather than completing rote, or canned, lab exercises. Schools with sufficient funds may set up a designated makerspace lab within the school. Makerspaces may be outside the school, within the home, family, or community. There might be a makerspace in the local library or science museum. A parent teaching his or her child to cook, fix the car, or build a birdhouse or model airplane is serving as a mentor in a makerspace.

Wherever they are, makerspaces are intergenerational, interdisciplinary, and innovative. One thing all educators agree on is that makerspaces are powerful. They open students to opportunities, stimulate their innate desires to use their brains and their hands, and fuel their curiosity and creativity. Students in makerspaces transform from passive consumers of knowledge into active learners, innovators, and problem solvers. Teachers are mentors, and students are at the center of the learning process.

WHAT SCHOOL MAKERSPACES DO

According to makerspace expert John Spencer, many teachers have been using makerspaces for years. Spencer teaches university

and online courses about makerspaces, design thinking, and project-based learning. He says the key to a maker-space is that students are actually creating a product. It could be digital (say, a computer program) or physical (say,

After the hard work of designing and building their robot, these students are trying it out. Perfecting it will likely require many tweaks and trials.

a robot), but it must involve making something. Designing an event or a service project does not count. While both are worthwhile, they do not meet the goals of a makerspace.

The Castilleja School, a grades six-to-twelve girls' school in Palo Alto, California, has makerspaces designed for both middle and high school students. The middle school area, called the Middle School Tinkering Nook, is located in the open lobby of the middle school building. Students are invited to come and tinker, to have fun while solving design and engineering problems in a low-pressure environment. The more formal Bourn Idea Lab houses Castilleja's engineering design studio and robotics lab. This lab has a variety of digital tools, shop tools, and materials. Here, students turn their design ideas into prototypes. The lab places special emphasis on practicing spatial reasoning skills, a key skill used in STEM careers.

Both middle and high school students at Castilleja build robots and participate in robotics competitions. Middle school students build LEGO robots and participate in the FIRST LEGO League Competition. High school students participate in a new robotics challenge every year in the FIRST Robotics Competition. They may specialize in mechanical engineering, electronics, programming, or entrepreneurship. Students are mentored by professionals in the robotics industry.

Makerspaces at the college and university level are more intensive. At Carnegie Mellon University in Pittsburgh, Pennsylvania, the robotics makerspace is the Carnegie Mellon Robotics Club, or Roboclub. This student organization combines a makerspace with a social space. It is open 24/7 when school is in session, and students use it to do

MAKERSPACES AT HOME

Every parent can set up a home makerspace for his or her children, beginning when they are very young. The materials can be household items such as paper towel rolls, containers and lids, cardboard, and ribbon. Other materials are easily available: LEGOs, pipe cleaners, aluminum foil, wire, glue guns, and art supplies such as crayons, markers, and paints. Tape, glue, and scissors are also essential. There should be a storage area and a space nearby where kids can work. Kids should help design and set up their own makerspace and be responsible for keeping it neat. Changing or adding supplies occasionally can keep things fresh and help generate new ideas. The key is to stimulate kids' imaginations and their natural inclination to invent and create. As Thomas Edison, quoted on the Modular Robotics website, said, "To invent, you need a good imagination and a pile of junk."

robotics projects for classes, for clubs, or just for fun. Here, university students build robots from scratch, using shop tools such as mills, lathes, and drills; hand tools such as saws, clamps, and screwdrivers; electrical test equipment; and materials ranging from wires to electronic parts. The lab also has a laser cutter and two types of 3D printers.

The Robotics Club makerspace is managed by a team of graduate and undergraduate officers. They maintain equipment, set up events, find sponsors, and keep the area clean. Every semester, the club offers training sessions in electronics, programming, tool usage, and 3D printing. Members work on club-sponsored robot projects, including flying robots, cooking robots, and musical robots. Others work on personal robot projects. Because membership is open to all majors, Roboclub is highly interdisciplinary.

GOALS OF A MAKERSPACE

Laura Fleming, author of the book *Worlds of Making: Best Practices for Establishing a Makerspace for Your School*, states that rather than becoming fixated on equipment and technology, a makerspace should focus on the four Cs: creativity, critical thinking, communication, and collaboration. In particular, harnessing students' creativity will develop their ability to innovate and help them get the most benefit from a makerspace.

Fleming lists nine targets to strive for in a makerspace. These targets will narrow the focus of activities so they are not only enjoyable and fun but also highly productive and meaningful. Fleming's nine objectives are for students to do the following:

- Use a broad range of methods of idea creation, including brainstorming.
- Create new, worthwhile ideas.
- Develop, refine, analyze, and evaluate ideas.
- Effectively develop, implement, and communicate

Precise measurement and drawing skills are required for the design of any project, from robots to houses. Such skills are useful in any maker-space or real-world project.

new ideas to others.
- Be open to new perspectives, and incorporate group input and feedback.
- Show inventiveness and originality, and understand the limits of new ideas in the real world.
- Accept failure as an opportunity to learn, and understand that creativity and innovation are long-term, cyclical processes that involve both successes and failures.
- Implement innovations.
- Act on creative ideas to make useful contributions to the relevant field.

A makerspace can be simple and inexpensive or complex and expensive. It may use everyday materials or up-to-date technologies. Much more than the amount of money invested, the key to a successful makerspace lies in the mind-set of its mentors and participants. Eventually, students who plan to enter a high-tech field such as robotics will need to master high-tech equipment. But many key skills needed to work in such fields—such as systems thinking, judgment and decision making, good communication, complex problem solving, and above all, persistence—can be learned with the simplest materials and equipment in the smallest of makerspaces.

CHAPTER TWO

FROM MAKERSPACES TO ROBOTICS CAREERS

When elementary or middle school students make their first robot from a kit, they are probably just having fun. But this first makerspace experience, whether it occurs in a classroom, a science museum, or one's own living room, can be the foundation for an exciting future career. Students from kindergarten to graduate school can use the skills learned in robotics makerspaces for a lifetime. More and more students are also using robots to learn math, science, and other educational content. This trend is expected to increase in the future. In short, robots are rapidly becoming part of the fabric of our society.

COMPUTATIONAL THINKING

A major goal of teaching robotics is helping students develop computational thinking—a skill valuable not only

These young roboticists used computational thinking to design their robot. Computational thinking is a STEM skill that requires students to express problems logically or mathematically.

for roboticists, but for all thinkers—that is, all humans. Jeannette Wing, corporate vice president of Microsoft Research, gives a precise definition of computational thinking. In an article for the blog *Social Issues in Computing*, she defines it as "the thought processes involved in formulating a problem and expressing its solution(s) in such a way that a computer—human or machine—can effectively carry out." Wing deliberately uses the terms *expressing* and *effectively* as technical terms. By *expressing*, she refers to the use of precise programming language to define the problem and communicate the solution to others. The word *effectively* indicates that, depending on the precision of the language in the computer program, the solution can be either elegant or inelegant—that is, straightforward or messy.

Computational thinking follows, in order, a three-step process: abstraction, analysis, and automation. According to Wing, abstraction, or formulating the problem, is key to the process. Abstraction is the thought process by which a person learns to define patterns, generalize from specific instances, and deal with complexity. Until the learner understands this process, analysis and automation are not possible. Analysis involves considering the problem and forming and evaluating a solution. Automation is the actual expression of the solution. Computer science, according to texts in the field, is the automation of abstractions—a computer program allows the person to carry out the solution to an abstract problem that has been defined and analyzed.

Consider a simple example: a student wants to build a robot that can avoid objects. The problem, or abstraction, is that the robot must be able to sense and avoid any object in its path—not just a single object. Through analysis, the student concludes that the robot must be able to recognize that the path ahead is not clear. This might suggest, for example, that a sensor must recognize when light is blocked. This, in turn, would involve placement of the robot's light sensor. The nearer to the floor the sensor is placed, the smaller the object that could be detected. The robot must also be able to carry out an action to avoid the object. Finally, the student writes a computer program to solve both of these problems—to enable the robot to first

A participant designs an illustrated panel for a presentation called The Frontiers of Computational Thinking at the 2015 SXSW Music, Film + Interactive Festival in Austin, Texas.

sense, and then avoid, the object in its path. Using computational thinking, the student has carried out the three processes of abstraction, analysis, and automation.

HOW ROBOTS ARE TEACHING KIDS

Robots teach young kids through play. While interacting with robots, kids absorb programming, building, and STEM skills without even being aware they are learning. They learn basic computational thinking. This enables them to program robots to do increasingly complex tasks. Robots already being used in classrooms include programmable

REAL-WORLD ROBOT DESIGN

Dr. Ayanna Howard is a robotics engineer at NASA. She teaches robots—specifically, Mars rovers—to travel long distances on Mars. *Sojourner*, an early rover, used very simple logic, Howard says. When it approached a rock, it stopped and then turned left or right. Her rovers have more intelligence and use more complex logic. Her goal is to show a rover a mountain in the distance and have it navigate by itself and reach the mountain in a given time frame, say overnight. Howard writes software for robot navigation and tests it on models of rovers in her lab. The rovers will eventually have cameras panning all 360 degrees of the terrain.

LEGO bricks and the Pi-Bot, a middle school kit that lets students assemble and program their own robot.

A pair of small robots named Bo and Yana, now renamed Dash and Dot, are sold by a company called the Wonder Workshop. Bo and Yana connect wirelessly using Bluetooth 4.0 with mobile devices, including Apple iOS and Google Android. Bo consists of four interconnected spheres, which kids can program to glide over the floor. It avoids obstacles and delivers items. Yana is a single sphere covered with sensors. Kids can program the two robots to carry out various tasks, such as hide-and-seek, racing, and solving a maze. Interactions are open ended; kids decide what to do with the robots. The process combines learning and fun.

The company RobotLAB makes robots for high school students. Students learn math and programming skills by programming the ready-made robots to carry out various functions. NAO is a fully programmable, minihumanoid robot with a variety of sensors. The RobotLAB BOX provides real-world experiences to supplement math and science curricula. It consists of a tablet computer with fifty lesson plans and four robots with different abilities: the AR.Drone (flying), the ArmBot (stationary arm), Sphero (rolling ball), and the Mobot (mobile).

Two other companies provide systems that enable older students to make their own robots. With EZ-Robot, students make and program new robots using open-source software and hardware. They can share their creations with other EZ-Robot users. The software has a graphical user interface, such as Windows, to assist beginning robot makers. Students with access to 3D printers can print parts for their robots.

Linkbots are modules that can be snapped together and customized to make a variety of types of robots. The two main Linkbot modules have accelerometers—instruments for measuring acceleration—and they connect wirelessly. Students can move one module to control the other, similar to using a Nintendo Wii controller. For simple programming, students manipulate the robot with their hands instead of giving it computer instructions. They write programs to carry out more complex movements.

FROM MAKERSPACE TO CAREER

The Sierra College Robotics Club, one of the college's makerspaces, participates in many robotics competitions. In April 2018, the club won second place in RoboGames, held in Pleasanton, California, for its Autonomous Firefighter robot. The robot could locate and extinguish a burning candle in a scale model of a house. According to Sierra College instructor Tony Osladil, competitions help prepare students for future careers. The students use industry-standard hardware and equipment, he says. They learn essential soft skills, including time management, budgeting, and teamwork. One supporter of the club is TSI Semiconductors of Roseville, California. According to Nancy Shafer, TSI's senior human resources representative, the company has hired many of the club's graduates.

ROBOTS IN FUTURE SCHOOLS

Present-day robots are mainly used to teach programming and robotics and to help students understand math and science concepts. But robot use in tomorrow's schools may be more complex and pervasive. Unusual uses of robots are already happening in some schools. Students unable to attend school are using robots as friends and partners in education. When Tyler Gibson was undergoing chemotherapy for cancer, he kept up with his schoolwork—and

Lexie Kinder of Sumter, South Carolina, has been unable to attend school for nearly two years. Teacher Ivey Smith now talks to Lexie from the classroom using the VGo robot.

saw his classmates—using the VGo robot, which he could control from home. VGo enabled him to see and hear what was happening in the classroom and even wave to his classmates.

Students with autism have trouble communicating with people. They do not understand facial expressions and non-verbal cues. Humanoid robots, such as the NAO, can help autistic students learn social cues and can also help them with regular classroom learning. Using the NAO, young children have learned to identify different types of animals, and older students have learned basic reading skills. Robots are even helping with distance learning. Long-distance students no longer just see and hear the teacher. Now, teachers' voices and actions are streamed through a tablet, which a robot carries around to the students, so student and teacher can interact directly.

In 2018, these educational robots were relatively expensive and not available to all students. But as prices decline, they will become increasingly available. Experts predict that, as distance learning becomes more common, robots will aid in the transition from classroom to long-distance student-teacher contact.

Aspiring roboticists can start building robots in elementary school and continue to expand and hone their skills all the way through college. They may use robots in everyday learning experiences and build them in the school's makerspaces. Competitions will provide the chance to see if their creations measure up in real-world situations. Every skill they learn, from building electronic circuits to getting along with teammates, will benefit them as they enter robotics careers.

CHAPTER THREE

HOME AND MEDICAL ROBOTICS CAREERS

People need the same basic knowledge to build and program any type of robot. But most robotics fields will also require specialized skills and knowledge. For example, a person interested in developing microbots to cure cancer will require medical as well as robotics training. A person's interests will determine the direction he or she follows in a robotics career—and the directions seem almost infinite.

HOME AND SERVICE ROBOTS

Many people are familiar with the Roomba, iRobot's robotic vacuum cleaner. Sometimes, Roomba trundles randomly around the house, sucking up dirt. Sometimes, it follows the walls and cleans the corners of a room. It even plugs itself in for recharging. But, despite the robots in science fiction that cook, clean, and take care of the kids, Roomba is one

The Roomba robotic vacuum was unveiled in 2002. iRobot also builds robotic systems for the US Department of Defense, the military, law enforcement, and other industries.

of the few household robots so far that has made it big in the real world. The Dyson 360 Eye, launched in the United Kingdom in 2018, is similar. Like the newest Roombas, it

BUILDING SERVICE ROBOTS

Dr. Tessa Lau describes herself as chief robot whisperer at Savioke. This robotics company builds autonomous robot helpers for the service industry. Lau has a bachelor's degree in applied physics and computer science and a PhD in artificial intelligence and human-computer interactions. She makes sure robots behave well with people. One of her skills, she says, is soft leadership—making sure team members work together seamlessly. She says team members must know a little about many things but also have areas of specialty.

Lau thinks robots will fundamentally change our lives. They will not take people's jobs, she says, because humans can do so much more. Instead, robots will do mundane tasks that humans don't want to do. One type of Savioke robot works in a hotel. When a guest calls the front desk to order a sandwich, the clerk places the sandwich inside a compartment on the robot and types in the room number. The robot delivers the sandwich to the correct room. The team can log in to the service robots over the internet and watch as they make deliveries and interact with hotel guests. Guests are delighted. "All of those interactions are happening because of things that I built," says Lau. "That's really incredible."

uses lasers and cameras to map rooms and plot an optimum route to make sure everything is cleaned completely.

Personal-assistant robots for the home and service industries are still in the early stages. Zenbo, made by Asus, was released in 2016. Zenbo has several cameras and can move through a house without bumping into walls. A touchscreen face enables it to show emotion. With speakers and microphones, it responds to voice commands and chats with humans. It is said to control home appliances, read a recipe, detect and react to emergencies, and tell the kids a story. Zenbo is meant to function as a smart home hub that controls other devices, similar to Amazon's Echo. But as of early 2019, it had not become available in the United States.

HOME ROBOTICS EXPANDS

Amazon is already a leader in the smart home control market with its Alexa-Echo combination. Alexa uses the Echo wireless speaker system, which also enables the user to carry out other actions, such as turning on lights, playing music, making a to-do list, or getting a weather report. Although a smartphone will also do these things, the Alexa system is ideal for home use because it responds to voice commands. It lets users control any Alexa-compatible home device without launching an app. Users can even write their own small programs, or apps, to teach Alexa additional activities. However, Alexa is not technically a robot, because it is stationary.

Amazon's Vesta works with Alexa when the two systems are integrated. Vesta is a small robot, similar to Zenbo, which will move around the house and carry out commands from Alexa. For example, a user might say, "Alexa, tell Vesta to turn on living room lights," or "Alexa, tell Vesta I'm in danger." Vesta has computer vision software and advanced camera technology and will move similar to the way self-driving cars move. As of early 2019, Amazon had not shared details of Vesta's design or function. But the company was hiring many new engineers specializing in software for robotics and sensors.

Play music, read audiobooks, answer calls, check messages, set alarms, answer questions, adjust thermostats—whatever people need, Amazon's Echo-Alexa, a smart home system, can do it using voice commands.

Other companies, including Sony and LG Electronics, are also funding secret projects to design home robots. Mark Gurman, in the *Seattle Times*, quotes Gene Munster, cofounder of Loup Ventures: "Robots are the next big thing." The US home robot market, according to Munster, will quadruple to $4 billion by 2025. Home robots are still in the early stages, but advances in artificial intelligence (AI), voice recognition, computer vision, and sensors suggest that home robotics will be an up-and-coming source of robotics jobs.

ROBOTS IN MEDICINE

The world of medical robots is wide and growing. Robots will soon be members of the medical staff in hospitals across the country. Some are already at work. The Xenex robot uses UV light to disinfect hospital rooms and surfaces, decreasing deadly hospital infections. The TUG robot can carry up to 1,000 pounds (454 kilograms) of medical supplies. Medical personnel use its touch screen to send it anywhere in the hospital. RIBA, or Robot for Interactive Body Assistance, specializes in patient care. It lifts and moves patients, helps them stand, and turns them to prevent bedsores. Veebot makes drawing blood easier. It examines the patient's veins, selects the best one, and draws blood in less than a minute.

The da Vinci Surgical System, made by Intuitive Surgical, employs magnified 3D high-definition vision and tiny instruments that rotate much more freely than the human hand. It helps surgeons operate much more precisely, using just a few small incisions. Da Vinci's success has encouraged other companies to invest in research on surgical helpers. As of 2019, such robots were assistants only, completely controlled by doctors. But, as AI improves, roboticists expect robotic surgical systems to develop more autonomy in the operating room. None of these robots replaces medical professionals. Instead, they improve patient care while making medical jobs easier, safer, and more efficient.

Germany's Max Planck Institute is researching micro-bots—tiny robots less than 1 millimeter across—that swim through a patient's bloodstream and target medi-cations or other therapies directly to the cells that need

ROBOTS FOR KIDS

Marek Michalowski is cofounder of the company Beat-Bots, which creates small, interactive robots for chil-dren. One of BeatBots' robots is Keepon, a small, yellow, birdlike robot composed of two furry balls. Keepon interacts with autistic children. It has cameras in its eyes and a microphone in its nose. A therapist con-trols the robot from another room, so the therapist can interact with the child through the simpler body. Other BeatBot robots are used in research, entertainment, ed-ucation, and art. The most rewarding aspect of his work, says Michalowski, is bringing his robots into the world and seeing children's reactions to them.

them. Microbots can be printed on 3D printers. These tiny, advanced medical robots are still in the research stages, but they could soon revolutionize the treatment of many diseases, including cancers. Microrobotics would be much less invasive than most modern medical techniques. Because microbots target only the affected area, treatments can use much lower doses of medication. But many challenges remain. Microbots must be nontoxic and biodegradable, and researchers must learn to track and control swarms of microbots inside the body. They must become autonomous, so they can find their own way to the target cells. These challenges mean plenty of work for future medical roboticists.

AI IN MEDICINE

IBM's Watson, an AI robot, is probably best known for beating two champions on the television show *Jeopardy!* Now, Watson is turning its skills to medicine, specifically complex medical decision making. Watson can collect, organize, and summarize as many as sixty million pages of text every second. It is being trained to attend patient examinations, listening and remembering. As it learns,

it gets better at understanding medical problems, making diagnoses, and recommending treatments. Watson lists a series of possible diagnoses or treatments and indicates its level of confidence for each.

In 2011, Watson, an AI robot, beat two *Jeopardy!* champions, Ken Jennings and Brad Rutter. Jennings acknowledged his defeat, saying, "I, for one, welcome our new computer overlords."

According to Marty Kohn, an emergency room physician and one of Watson's trainers, Watson's greatest value might lie in its ability to overcome human limitations. Kohn, quoted in an article by Jonathan Cohn in the *Atlantic*, states that all doctors make errors in treatment, one-third of which are caused by misdiagnosis. Doctors tend to focus on two or three symptoms and ignore other symptoms that might change the diagnosis. Or they make only a partial diagnosis. Watson considers all information; it does not make these mistakes. According to Kohn, Watson may be a potential medical game changer, preventing costly and dangerous errors in treatment.

Within a few decades, robots in homes, service industries, and hospitals will likely be routine. Home appliances and electronics will be connected and controlled by a smart hub, with one or more robots maintaining the systems—and probably interacting with the human occupants. Service robots will take over many mundane jobs. Medical robots, from microbots to large movers such as TUG, will both assist medical professionals and act autonomously. In the coming decades, robots will likely be a normal part of life.

CHAPTER FOUR

INDUSTRIAL AND MILITARY ROBOTICS CAREERS

In the near future, robots will largely do jobs people cannot or do not want to do. For example, robots are taking on repetitive jobs on factory assembly lines and other industrial jobs, including heavy lifting and stocking shelves. Robots also do dangerous jobs; they act as soldiers and handle hazardous materials. In this way, robots will make humans' lives easier and safer.

INDUSTRIAL ROBOTS

Today, robots are used in nearly every industry. They are especially prevalent in mining, manufacturing, the military, and health care. Industrial, or manufacturing, robots are automatically controlled and reprogrammable. Most are robot arms that can move on three or more axes and are designed with a tool on the end that performs a specific action. Robot arms differ in type of movement, also called

Industrial robots are designed according to their function. This factory's automated assembly line is used to make paper boxes or cartons.

degrees of freedom, and application, or the manufacturing process they carry out. For example, Cartesian robots move in three directions, or three translations, called x, y, and z. SCARA robots do three translations and rotate around a vertical arm, and 6-axis robots can position their tool based on three positions and three orientations. In addition, dual-arm robots have two arms that work together.

Applications, or jobs robot arms do, include welding, materials handling, palletizing (placing items on pallets), painting, assembly, cutting, finishing, spraying, sealing, and gluing. Some of these applications, such as welding and

ROBOT OR HUMAN: WHO'S IN CHARGE?

Many people worry that robots will take over human jobs, or perhaps even worse, people will end up working for robots. British computer scientist and web expert Wendy Hall, in an interview with *Green European Journal*, points out that computers have already taken over many types of jobs. All calculators, for example, used to be humans. Hall expects the future to follow the trend seen in science fiction, where robots essentially manage human lives. Although the robots may not be intelligent, robot companies will hire many low-wage human workers to do jobs the robots cannot do. But an article in the online magazine Acculturated emphasizes that robots cannot do what makes us human. They expertly manage huge masses of data, but they cannot make value judgments or understand the data's human implications. A robot doctor might analyze a patient's symptoms and diagnose her cancer. However, the robot will not see cancer as a bad thing or recognize the patient's fear. It will not care if she lives or dies.

Entrepreneur Steven Rosenbaum, writing for *Forbes*, is concerned with robots passing themselves off as humans. He cites the "tweet bot" on Twitter that responds "Thanks for following me." He cannot tell if the response comes from a human or from a robot mimicking or impersonating a human. Rosenbaum proposes a new rule of robotics: "Robots must identify themselves as robots—and can't impersonate a human being."

painting, are dangerous. Materials handling may involve hazardous materials, including chemicals. Industry experts see robots as highly valuable to the industry because they help prevent accidents, leading to a safer workplace. Robots can also make industrial processes run faster and more reliably, which improves productivity.

The next generation of industrial robots is likely to be collaborative robots. They will work alongside humans in factories. According to data from Loup Ventures, a venture capital firm, as reported by Recode, collaborative robots made up only 3 percent of robots sold in 2016, but by 2025, they will make up 34 percent. The overall market for industrial robots will grow by 175 percent. Collaborative robots are still robot arms. They cost less than traditional robots, are smaller, and have more sensors. They react faster and with more intelligence. Use of collaborative robots is expected to rise in automobile manufacturing, where they are now most common. They will also increase in electronics and medical device manufacturing. The demand for new and better robots is rising rapidly. Future robotics experts will be part of designing, building, and pro-gramming robots that will do tomorrow's manufacturing.

MILITARY ROBOTS

The military has used robots in warfare since World War II, when the Germans deployed Goliath, a remote-controlled robot carrying 200 pounds (91 kg) of explosives to destroy tanks, buildings, bridges, and people. The Soviet Union used Teletanks, remote-controlled tanks equipped with machine guns, flamethrowers, and smoke-bomb containers. Since then, the field of military robotics has exploded. The US military is investing huge amounts of money in robots. Militaries around the world consider automated robots the next big advance in warfare. According to the website Robots and Androids, military robots ignore—even destroy—Isaac Asimov's Three Laws of Robotics. Asimov's laws were designed to prevent robots from harming humans. But military robots, the website says, have three goals: "to monitor, to destroy property and to kill people."

In June 1944, on Normandy Beach, sailors from the US Navy observe a Goliath tracked mine, a beetle-shaped robot that was remotely controlled by Nazi forces.

Unmanned aerial vehicles, also called UAVs or drones, have been researched since the 1980s. UAVs fly without a human crew and mostly carry out reconnaissance but can also run attack missions. They range in size from handheld model airplanes to full-sized aircraft. One UAV, the MQ-1 Predator, carries cameras, other sensors, and missiles, which it has fired over countries including Afghanistan, Iraq, Pakistan, and Bosnia.

Another popular type of military robot is the unmanned ground vehicle, or UGV. Most UGVs have a head end, four articulated legs, and many sensors, similar to big dogs. In fact, one is called BigDog. The size of a pack mule, Big-Dog can carry up to 340 pounds (154 kg). It can climb a 35-degree incline and walk or run up to 4 miles (6.4 kilo-meters) per hour. Its legs are articulated like a real animal's,

ROBOTS ON MARS

Robots have been roving over the Martian surface since 2001. Rovers maneuver their way around rocks and sand dunes, heading for specific locations programmed in by their Earth-based handlers. Their sensors measure characteristics of the Martian atmosphere and soil and look for signs of water and life. As of 2018, Mars had two operational rovers, *Opportunity* and *Curiosity*. Before humans land on Mars, robots will build housing and laboratories for them. Astronauts will control the robots from an orbiting space station. They are already practicing by controlling Earth-based robots from the International Space Station. Data and video transmission are lost when an orbiting station is on the opposite side of the planet. When astronauts lose contact with their robots, this can jeopardize the building task or damage the robot. The UNISONO project, coordinated by VTT Technical Research Centre in Finland, is developing a communication system that enables an orbiting space station to have uninterrupted contact with robots on the planet's surface.

The *Curiosity* rover is part of the NASA Mars Science Laboratory mission. In this artist's depiction, *Curiosity* uses its sensors to investigate a rock surface.

so it can move over uneven ground and through snow, rain, ice, and mud.

TALON, a UGV made by Foster-Miller, weighs less than 100 pounds (45 kg), runs on treads, and has seven speeds, with a top speed of 6 feet (1.8 meters) per second. It is controlled by a joystick and can adapt to different situations. TALON was used for search and rescue when the World Trade Center fell in 2001. It has been used in Afghanistan and Iraq to dispose of live grenades and improvised explosive devices. There are even UUVs, or unmanned underwater vehicles, similar to tiny submarines, which carry out tasks such as mine warfare, intelligence, surveillance, and reconnaissance.

Previously, recruits practiced on pop-up or stationary targets. The first time they shot at a live target was on the battlefield. Marathon Targets, an Australian company, has developed AI robots that react like human targets and can train military recruits how to shoot at live targets. Like self-driving cars, they orient themselves using light detection and ranging (lidar) sensors. They run to rescue wounded "comrades." If hit in a vital organ, they fall over, but if only wounded, they come after the shooter.

THE FUTURE OF MILITARY ROBOTS

Researchers have big plans for future military robots. Marathon, for example, is considering robot medics that will pull wounded soldiers out of firefights and robots that can navigate tunnels and other dangerous underground spaces. The July 2018 rescue of twelve boys and their

Rescue personnel wait at a Thai cave entrance for news of the twelve trapped boys and their soccer coach in 2018. Robots could have led to a safer, faster rescue.

coach from a cave in Thailand would have been much easier with such robots. Many experts think that, in the near future, soldiers from rich countries will fight wars without ever coming into contact with enemy combatants. Robots will do reconnaissance and patrolling and will kill the enemy—all while being controlled from a distance. Those who favor robot use think that such robots will decrease battlefield casualties and will not make errors or suffer from fatigue or emotion. But there are concerns. Some think that, if US soldiers are less likely to be killed, US citizens may become more tolerant of our government engaging in wars overseas. Also, when two countries engage in a robots-only conflict, how is the winner determined?

In 2015, thousands of scientists and technologists signed an open letter calling for a ban on the use of artificial intelligence to control lethal weapons. They cite both practical and ethical reasons. Some think AI will never advance to the point that a robot can become fully autonomous, but others fear that, as AI advances, people might lose control over robots, resulting ultimately in rogue killer robots. But aside from this fear, many people feel the use of robots instead of humans in war is unethical, especially when only one side has access to them.

As the robotics industry matures, new ethical dilemmas will unfold, leading to another potential career direction. Some people might like robotics but prefer soft sciences more than designing, building, programming, and operating robots. These people may consider jobs in which they study the effects of robot use on psychology, ethics, or society.

CHAPTER FIVE

PREPARING FOR A ROBOTICS CAREER

Robotics careers vary, based on the amount of education required and the field in which the robots are being used. In general, people working directly with robots specialize in either engineering or computer science, and sometimes both. Engineering majors will primarily design, build, or operate robots. Some will be technicians who test or repair them. Computer science majors will program robots, writing instructions to make them do certain tasks. Typical robotics job titles include robotics engineer, robotics technician, robotics operator, and software developer. Those with robotics knowledge and excellent people skills might excel as sales engineers or sales account managers. These careers involve selling robotic systems or related technologies, keeping accounts, and doing customer service. Still others might choose research or teaching careers

German robotics engineer Hannes Eilers shows off Emma, a robot he programmed to help dementia sufferers. Emma speaks, plays music, and takes photographs.

as high school science teachers, university professors, or researchers in private companies.

SKILLS AND EDUCATION

Anyone interested in robotics should be a lifelong learner. Robotics changes so rapidly that those in the field must learn constantly just to keep up with the latest advances. Robotics is a highly interdisciplinary field, so good roboticists likely have wide-ranging interests. They must know at least a little bit about everything related to robotics.

During their youth, they should develop many skills and become good at many different things. This involves both mental skills, such as solving puzzles, mysteries, or math problems, and physical, or hands-on skills, such as fixing a car, building a model airplane, or putting together a drone or automated car from a kit.

In high school and middle school, everyone who aspires to a robotics career should become well grounded in two key subjects: mathematics and science. Algebra and geometry are particularly key to all robotics fields. All sciences are useful

Aspiring roboticists should develop as many hands-on skills as possible. They should have fun tinkering and building.

HEATHER KNIGHT, SOCIAL ROBOTICIST

Dr. Heather Knight tries to create social interactions between robots and humans. She wants her robots to be charismatic. For example, a partygoer might have a robot companion that could remember everyone's name, help start conversations, and smooth over awkward pauses in conversation. Knight is an assistant professor of computer science at Oregon State University and director of the CHARISMA Research Lab. "CHARISMA" stands for "Collaborative Humans and Robots: Interaction, Sociability, Machine Learning, and Art." Knight researches topics such as human-robot interactions and nonverbal robot communications. She also teaches a course in social and ethical issues in computer science.

In an interview with *Magenta*, Knight says, "I got hooked on seeing people who knew nothing about robots discover them." She started by building a robot flower garden but quickly gravitated to theater and acting, which provide a long-term interactive experience. For example, a robot interacting with humans in an assisted living facility or a service industry must deal with relationships over time. Since 2010, Knight has also done stand-up comedy using her sidekick, Ginger the Robot. As a PhD candidate at Carnegie Mellon University, Knight created a robot theater company, Marilyn Monrobot, starring Ginger. The company also has an annual Robot Film Festival. Knight has continued the Marilyn Monrobot company in Oregon.

because they involve applying mathematics to real-world problems. Physics is especially valuable because it deals with energy, electricity, mechanics, materials science, and other key areas in robotics. Other courses to take during high school, if available, include courses in computer science or information systems, design and technology courses such as graphic communications or manufacturing, and any type of engineering course. This might include things like automotive engineering, bioengineering, mechanical engineering, or electronics.

Robotics is highly interdisciplinary, and many college paths can lead to a robotics career. Some colleges and universities have dedicated robotics degrees. However, according to roboticist Alex Owen-Hill, writing for Robotiq, most people follow a college path that concentrates on one of three aspects: the body, nervous system, or brain of the robot. Those interested in the robot's body might major in mechanical engineering, which looks at physical aspects such as mechanics and materials. They will concentrate on physical design and manufacture of the robot. Those interested in the nervous system will go into electrical or electronics engineering. Parts of this major involving robots will concentrate on automation, or control of robots, rather than design. Finally, the brain of the robot involves computer science. The programmer designs the algorithms and writes the software that makes the physical hardware and electronic systems work. Now and in the future, this career choice will involve artificial intelligence. The "brain" field, in particular, attracts graduate students from other fields, such as psychology, cognitive science, and pure mathematics.

Aspiring roboticists should definitely take advantage of robotics makerspaces in or out of school. In middle school, high school, and college, they should participate in robotics makerspaces, robotics clubs, or other groups—for example, science clubs—where robots, electronics, pro-gramming, or similar activities are done. They should do as many extracurricular activities involving robots as possible. These might involve museum groups or summer camps in which participants can make robots from kits, participate in robotics competitions, or otherwise get hands-on experience.

MAJORS, DEGREES, AND ACCREDITATION

A college education is required to work in the robotics industry. At least a two-year associate's degree and ideally a four-year bachelor's degree are the minimum requirements for positions such as robotics technician. A bachelor's degree is always required to work as a robotics engineer. Robotics technicians assist robotics engineers in the design, development, production, testing, and operation of robots. They install, maintain, and repair robots. Robotics

engineers may design robots for specific purposes and industries or may maintain robots in these areas. Robotics engineers and technicians are commonly employed in

Robotics engineers and technicians must have a thorough grounding in mathematics and the sciences.

industries such as automobile manufacture, aerospace, agriculture, security and defense, animatronics, and computer design organizations.

An associate's degree requires basic courses in math, physics, and engineering, including lab work in which students work with robotic components and learn programming, fabrication, and orientation processes. A bachelor's degree builds on this basic education, involving students in practical projects in areas such as mechanical, electrical, operational, and construction engineering. Some bachelor's degrees are in specialized areas of engineering, such as computer science or mechanical engineering. A specific bachelor's degree in robotics engineering integrates many engineering fields and develops skills needed to invent and modify robots and AI systems. In addition to engineering courses, the degree requires courses in physics, calculus, computer engineering, technology in society, robotics engineering ethics, and trends in robotics.

Many excellent career opportunities are available with a bachelor's degree. Master's and PhD degrees in robotics and related fields are also available. In addition to lecture and lab work, these graduate programs require individual thesis projects. Students specialize in an area of robotics, perhaps AI, perception, control systems, or robot design. Their courses and thesis project are planned around this specialization. They may also complete apprenticeships at robotics companies.

Licensing and certification are not required in the robotics field, but certification is available. FANUC is the leading international company in automation for manufacturing.

FANUC America offers four certifications: Certified Robot Operator 1 and 2 certify a person's ability to hold an entry-level position in robot operation. Certified Robot Technician 1 and 2 certify understanding at a higher level, involving technical aspects of operations, programming, and robot system components. Level 1 in both certifications requires passing a written exam; Level 2 is a performance, or skills, assessment. The Society of Manufacturing Engineers offers the Certified Manufacturing Engineering credential. Applicants must first meet education and work require-ments. Then, they must pass the Integration and Control exam, which deals primarily with AI and computer-aided manufacturing.

JOB OUTLOOK, PAY, AND WORKING CONDITIONS

In the *Occupational Outlook Handbook* of the Bureau of Labor Statistics, the occupation closest to robotics engineer is mechanical engineer. For 2017, mechanical engineers made a median salary of $85,880 per year when entering the field with a bachelor's degree. The field is expected to grow by 9 percent between 2016 and 2026, adding about 25,300 jobs. There is no specific information for the robotics specialty. How-ever, because robotics is a rapidly growing industry, it is safe to assume that a person trained in robotics will be well placed to start the career he or she is seeking. Mechanical engineering technicians with an associate's degree made a median salary of $55,360 in 2017.

Mechanical engineers, including robotics engineers, analyze problems and research and design sensors and devices to solve these problems. They spend much of their time in offices, working on computers and using computer-assisted design technology. They work in labs, where they build and test prototypes of their designs. They may investigate and analyze equipment problems and failures in already operating equipment. Mechanical engineering technicians assist engineers in all of these tasks. The outlook for robotics careers, at all levels, looks bright.

CHAPTER SIX

FINDING A JOB IN ROBOTICS

After completing your formal education, the next step is to find your dream job in robotics. Finding a job involves the same steps, regardless of the field. First, locate jobs you would like and that fit your qualifications. Second, write a cover letter and a résumé. Prepare a portfolio of your best work, if appropriate. Locate and contact people willing to serve as references. Deliver or send your job applications and wait for interview requests to come in. Prepare well for interviews, and send a thank-you letter after each interview. After being offered a job, negotiate salary and other terms. Finally, accept the job of your dreams and begin your exciting career in robotics.

JOB HUNTING

Even before looking for a job, prospective roboticists should consider exactly what type of job they want. This might

Thorough online research, especially through online job services, is a good way to find robotics jobs. You can also use online research to learn about potential employers.

involve asking people in the field about their jobs and doing online research. It is also important to take stock of one's qualifications. A person should be qualified for every job he or she applies for.

The first step in obtaining employment is locating jobs to apply for. Jobs are available from many sources, including word of mouth and social media contacts, newspaper ads, and online job services, including Indeed, LinkedIn, Monster, and ZipRecruiter. Job fairs are another good source. Liz Miller, writing for Learn Robotics, briefly outlines how to effectively pitch yourself to job-fair recruiters. She suggests writing a ten-second introduction, telling the recruiter your

WHAT ROBOTICS ENGINEERS DO

Robotics engineers spend most of their time designing parts for new robots and processes for running the robots. Creating a robot is painstaking and time consuming, taking years per robot. First, the engineer researches what the robot will do and determines the processes it will use. The design process itself involves a lot of thinking and using computer design programs. Robotics engineers also build, configure, and test robots. They constantly analyze prototypes, then evaluate, revise, and analyze them again. Robotics engineers serve as tech support for the robots they create. They may design software to control robots and teach these plans, or algorithms, to the robots. They may research, design, and test robot components or systems. In specific production industries, they may design robotic systems specifically to increase levels of production and precision.

first name, year in college, and goal—to obtain a job or internship in a specific area of robotics. Then, list the top ten companies you want to visit, research them, and circle them on a map of the job fair so they are easy to find. Take with you only essential items: a pen, legal pad, cell phone, job-fair map, résumés, and business cards. Finally, always ask questions, and send a thank-you note to every recruiter you visit.

An important new job-hunting tool is available from CareerBuilder, a company that uses the latest technology to help employers and employees find each other. CareerBuilder's mobile app is a full-service job-finding application for any mobile device. The mobile app uses maps to show available jobs in a specific area. Using augmented reality, it can also show available jobs in your immediate vicinity; for example, as you walk down the street. It builds and stores résumés on the spot and automatically applies for jobs. It can be set to notify you when your application is being viewed and by whom. It can also automatically apply for available jobs based on a list of companies you provide and notify you of available jobs as they are posted.

If you are interested in working for particular companies, study their websites and then contact their human resources departments for information about job openings. Ask for help from your college or university professors and job services. Finally, keep looking and keep applying. Do not get discouraged when you receive a rejection. Do not stop when you get an interview. Keep sending applications until you have signed on the dotted line.

COVER LETTERS AND RÉSUMÉS

Every job application requires a cover letter and a résumé. The cover letter introduces the applicant, so it should impress the prospective employer. It should never exceed one page and approximately four paragraphs. The first paragraph introduces you and states the job being applied

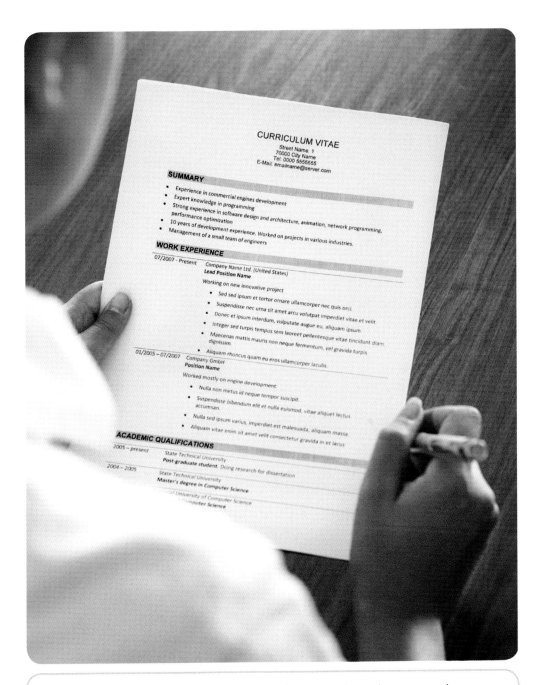

Most employers in the United States ask potential employees to submit résumés, but some may prefer a curriculum vitae—a longer, more detailed description of your work and education.

for and how you learned of it. The second briefly reviews your educational background, including college major and important awards or projects. The third summarizes your work background, stressing important skills or qualifications. It should show that you are responsible, reliable, and trustworthy and can work independently. The final paragraph should thank the employer and explain briefly why you would be the best candidate for the job. It should also provide contact information, such as a telephone number. The letter should explain the applicant's qualifications using keywords from the job advertisement. This information is covered in more detail in the résumé; the cover letter should hit the highlights.

A résumé is a two-page summary of a job applicant's credentials. It distills educational and work experience, goals, and accomplishments into easily readable bullet points. The applicant's name and contact information should appear at the top of each page. The first section should be a general goals statement; for example, "My goal is to work as a programmer in the field of robotics." After this, some résumés provide a short, bulleted list of skills. The next section should list education, beginning with the most recent school and working backward. Limit this to education applicable to the job, and list the dates and the qualification (for example, degree or certificate) obtained. The work experience section should list jobs starting with the most recent and should include apprenticeships. It should mention the level of responsibility attained—for example, did you open and close the business or supervise other employees? Finally, the résumé should introduce the applicant as a person. An accomplishment list could include awards, scholarships, or personal achievements. A hobbies list shows that you are a well-rounded person. At the end of the résumé, add "References upon Request" rather than listing references' names.

INTERVIEWS

Always prepare for an interview by learning everything you can about the company and the job. Be able to relate your own skills to the job requirements and to sell yourself as the best person for the job. Practice your answers to likely

On a job interview, it is important to make a good first impression. This can be as simple as a smile and a positive attitude. It also involves appropriate dress.

interview questions in advance. Create a portfolio of your past work and accomplishments. This could include photos or descriptions of robotics projects, awards, or other accomplishments. Have an easily accessible web page with the same information.

TYPICAL INTERVIEW QUESTIONS

Interview questions can never be predicted exactly, but many of the same questions—not related to robotics—pop up in all interviews. A well-prepared job seeker will prepare answers for these questions. Common questions include the following:

- What is your greatest strength (weakness)?
- Tell me about yourself.
- Where do you envision yourself in five years?
- What is your greatest accomplishment?
- What salary do you expect?
- Do you have any questions? (You should.)
- What experiences have you had that prepare you for this robotics job?
- Why do you want to work for our company?
- What do you know about our company?
- How well do you work under pressure?
- Describe a difficult situation you were in and how you handled it.
- How would you describe your work style?

Dress and act professionally for the interview. Be friendly and respectful. Answer the questions asked. Be self-confident and assured without being arrogant. Some questions may not cover your training or experience, but rather your personality and interests. The interviewer wants to judge how well you would fit with the team. Avoid criticizing previous employers or talking about your own mistakes. Show the interviewer your portfolio, but never leave it at an interview. Always send a thank-you note after an interview.

THE NEW ROBOTICS JOB

Before your first day, ask for reading material on the company and learn as much as you can. When you start, first figure out your job duties, get comfortable with the workplace, and become friendly with colleagues. Talk to your supervisor about communication style—should you email, message on some other platform, or appear in person with questions and updates? Get comfortable with the pace of work, and ask your supervisor for more (or less) work, as necessary. Don't be afraid to ask questions. But also, when necessary, be willing to take initiative and learn the basics on your own. Volunteer to do jobs no one else wants to do. Arrive early and leave late; this shows you are committed to the job and also provides time to get to know your new colleagues. Take time to learn the unwritten codes of conduct in the workplace; this will help you fit in.

There are also things to avoid as a new employee. Never lie. Never blame others for your mistakes. Never gossip. That is, always respect coworkers and supervisors. Always be helpful; do not have the attitude that "it's not my problem." Never ask coworkers to do your work for you. Always respect common areas, such as kitchens and break areas. Clean up after yourself. Always be on time and pre-pared for meetings. Overall, the best rule is to be a good workplace citizen.

Every new robotics employee—whether technician or engineer—is on the road to a new and exciting career. Roboticists will have an important place in the coming century. They will be among the people who will change technology, and if the field is handled ethically, they will profoundly change society for the better.

GLOSSARY

algorithm The set of rules followed in a problem-solving process, especially by a computer.

artificial intelligence Also called AI; computer systems with the ability to perform tasks usually requiring human intelligence, including speech recognition, visual perception, language translation, and decision making.

automation The creation and application of technology to replace humans in the control of production and delivery of goods and services; automation often uses robots.

autonomous Acting independently, or able to do so; an autonomous robot, for example, would make decisions and perform actions on its own, without directions from a human.

coding Writing computer programs, or computer code, which enables communication between humans and computers; sometimes used interchangeably with the term "programming."

collaborative robots Robots that work alongside humans as opposed to doing the entire job themselves; they are smaller and cheaper than current industrial robots and are expected to be the next generation of robots.

computational thinking The thought processes involved in formulating problems and expressing solutions so that a computer (either human or machine) can effectively carry them out.

cover letter A letter written to accompany a résumé when applying for a job; it is the job applicant's first chance to impress a potential employer.

degrees of freedom Types of movement in a robot, or number of directions in which it can move; 3 degrees of freedom represents movement in three directions, representing length, width, and height (x, y, and z).

hackerspace A space where a group of computer programmers works together to "hack," or analyze and understand, computer programs. Today, hackerspaces have become basically synonymous with makerspaces and are spaces where people can work on a variety of projects, both those that are computer based and those that involve physical tools.

makerspace A place that enables making, where people can create, solve problems, collaborate, and experiment.

microbots Also called microrobots; very tiny robots (less than 1 mm across) that are injected into the bloodstream, travel through the blood and lymphatic system, and deliver medicine or other treatments to targeted areas of the body.

résumé A formal, two-page summary of a job applicant's credentials; it includes sections for experience and skills, work history, education, and (if space permits) other related material, such as internships and professional memberships.

robotics The branch of technology involving the design, construction, operation, and application of robots.

smart home A home that has appliances, lighting, heat and air-conditioning, security systems, TVs, and other electronics that communicate with each other and are remotely controlled by a smartphone or other wireless device.

soft skills Personal characteristics, such as people skills, communication skills, and attitudes, that improve a person's ability to work well with others in a job setting.

STEAM An approach to education that advocates interdisciplinary learning and inquiry in science, technology, engineering, arts, and mathematics; the older version, STEM, did not include arts.

unmanned aerial vehicle Also called a UAV or drone; a flying robot, either remotely controlled or functioning autonomously by means of embedded software; it contains sensors and GPS, and if military, it may deploy missiles or other weapons.

FOR MORE INFORMATION

American Society of Mechanical Engineers (ASME)
2 Park Avenue
New York, NY 10016-5990
(800) 843-2763
Website: https://www.asme.org
Facebook: @ASME.org
Twitter: @ASMEdotorg
This international organization serves students and engineering professionals. The ASME support conferences
and competitions, and its website provides current engineering news. The robotics branch of the ASME provides
information and resources specifically for the biomedical
engineering community. It covers all aspects of the field,
including robotics in medicine.

Canadian Space Agency
John H. Chapman Space Centre
6767 Route de l'Aeroport
Saint-Hubert, QC J3Y 8Y9
Canada
(450) 926-4800
Website: http://www.asc-csa.gc.ca/eng/canadarm/default
.asp
Facebook: @CanadianSpaceAgency
Twitter and Instagram: @csa_asc
The Canadian Space Agency has become known for its
robotics technology and has several robots, including
Canadarm2 and Dextre on the International Space
Station. The agency's website includes information,
multimedia, and activities.

FIRST Robotics Canada
c/o Studica
7220 Pacific Circle
Mississauga, ON L5T 1V1
Canada
Website: http://www.firstroboticscanada.org
Facebook: @FIRSTRoboticsCanada
Twitter: @CANFIRST
This group's mission is to inspire Canadian elementary
and high school students to pursue studies in science,
technology, and engineering. It sponsors robotics
competitions, teaches coding, and instills skills in
communication, teamwork, and leadership.

International Federation of Robotics (IFR)
c/o Gudrun Litzenberger, General Secretary
Lyoner Str. 18
60528 Frankfurt am Main
Germany
+49 69-6603-1502
Website: https://ifr.org
Twitter: @IFR_Robots
The IFR connects members of the robotics industry,
research, and educational organizations around the
world. It provides statistics, stimulates research, and
helps link science and industry in the robotics industry.

NASA—The Robotics Alliance Project (RAP)
NASA Headquarters
300 E. Street SW, Suite 5R30
Washington, DC 20546
(202) 358-0001
Website: https://robotics.nasa.gov
Twitter: @NASA_RAP

NASA's RAP sponsors the FIRST Robotics Competition. Its website has links to other websites describing various robotics projects. It also has resources for students and educators.

Robotic Industries Association (RIA)
900 Victors Way, Suite 140
Ann Arbor, MI
(734) 994-6088
Website: https://www.robotics.org
Facebook: @Robotic-Industries-Association
Twitter: @RIA_robotics
The RIA's website, Robotics Online, provides information for engineers and others interested in robotics and automation. It includes news, case studies, job openings, an "Ask the Experts" forum, and more.

Society of Manufacturing Engineers (SME)
1000 Town Center, Suite 1910
Southfield, MI 48075
(313) 425-3000
Website: https://www.sme.org
Facebook: @SMEmfg
Twitter: @SME_MFG
SME members are manufacturing professionals, educators, and students. The organization provides students with workforce training and certification, mentorship programs, jobs, publications and events, networking opportunities, and more.

Cinnamon, Ian, Romi Kadri, and Fitz Tepper. *DIY Drones for the Evil Genius: Design, Build, and Customize Your Own Drones* (Evil Genius Series). New York, NY: McGraw-Hill Education TAB, 2016.

Cohen, Jacob. *Getting the Most out of Makerspaces to Build Robots* (Makerspaces). New York, NY: Rosen Publishing, 2015.

Cooper, James. *Inside Robotics* (The Geek's Guide to Computer Science). New York, NY: Rosen Publishing, 2019.

Gunkel, David J. *Robot Rights*. Cambridge, MA: MIT Press, 2018.

Hulick, Kathryn. *Robotics and Medicine* (Next-Generation Medical Technology). San Diego, CA: ReferencePoint Press, 2018.

Hulick, Kathryn. *Robotics Engineer* (Cutting Edge Careers). San Diego, CA: ReferencePoint Press, 2017.

Martin, Claudia. *Robotics in Nature* (Robot Pioneers). New York, NY: Greenhaven Publishing, 2018.

McKinnon, Peter. *Robotics: Everything You Need to Know About Robotics from Beginner to Expert*. CreateSpace Independent Publishing Platform, 2016.

Porterfield, Jason. *Robots, Cyborgs, and Androids* (Sci-Fi or STEM?). New York, NY: Rosen Publishing, 2019.

Rauf, Don. *Getting the Most out of Makerspaces to Build Unmanned Aerial Vehicles* (Makerspaces). New York, NY: Rosen Publishing, 2015.

Sobey, Ed. *Build Your Own Robot Science Fair Project* (Prize-Winning Science Fair Projects). New York, NY: Enslow Publishing, 2016.

BIBLIOGRAPHY

Campbell, A. "MakerSpace Magic … Robotics 101@
    GEC!" Gleneagles Ch'axáÿ Elementary, West
    Vancouver Schools, March 31, 2017. http://
    westvancouverschools.ca/gleneagles-elementary
    /makerspace-magic-robotics-101-gec.
Castilleja. "Maker Spaces." Retrieved September 13, 2018.
    https://www.castilleja.org/learning/experiential-learning
    /maker-spaces.
CCC Maker. "Sierra Robotics Team Uses Makerspace to
    Create Winning Robot." California Community Colleges,
    Sierra College Makerspaces, June 6, 2018. https://
    cccmaker.com/sierra-robotics-team-uses
    -makerspace-to-create-winning-robot.
CuriosityCommons. "Makerspaces: The Benefits." Retrieved
    August 5, 2018. https://curiositycommons.wordpress
    .com/makerspaces-the-benefits.
DA Custom Publishing. "Makerspaces, Drones, and
    Robotics: The Next Generation of STEM." *Web
    Seminar Digest*, December 2017. https://www
    .districtadministration.com/article/makerspaces
    -drones-and-robotics-next-generation-stem-learning.
Fleming, Laura. *Worlds of Making: Best Practices for
    Establishing a Makerspace for Your School* (Corwin
    Connected Educators Series). Thousand Oaks, CA:
    Corwin, 2015.
Geer, David. "4 Robots That Teach Children Science and
    Math in Engaging Ways." *Scientific American*, May 1,
    2014. https://www.scientificamerican.com/article/4-robots
    -that-teach-children-science-and-math-in-engaging-ways.

Gibbs, Samuel. "Five In-Home Robots That Could Change Your Life." *Guardian*, June 1, 2016. https://www .theguardian.com/technology/shortcuts/2016/jun/01 /five-in-home-robots-that-could-change-your-life.

Glaser, April. "The Industrial Robotics Market Will Nearly Triple in Less than 10 Years." Recode, June 22, 2017. https://www.recode.net/2017/6/22/15763106 /industrial-robotics-market-triple-ten-years-collaborative -robots.

GradSchoolHub. "What Types of Jobs Are in Robotics?" Retrieved August 8, 2018. https://www.gradschoolhub .com/faqs/what-types-of-jobs-are-in-robotics.

Hall, Wendy. "Who's in Charge Here? Humans in a Robot World." *Green European Journal*, May 4, 2018. https://www.greeneuropeanjournal.eu/whos-in -charge-here-humans-in-a-robot-world.

Learn.org. "How to Become a Robotic Engineer in 5 Steps." Retrieved August 8, 2018. https://learn.org/articles /Robotics_Engineering_Become_a_Robotics_Engineer _in_5_Steps.html.

Miller, Liz. "How to Get a Robotics Job." Learn Robotics, May 6, 2017. https://www.learnrobotics.org/blog /how-to-get-a-robotics-job.

Owen-Hill, Alex. "10 Essential Skills That All Good Robot- icists Should Have." Robotiq, January 5, 2016. https:// blog.robotiq.com/10-essential-skills-that-all-good -roboticists-have.

Owen-Hill, Alex. "What to Study for a Career in Robotics?" Robotiq, September 30, 2015. https://blog.robotiq .com/what-to-study-for-a-career-in-robotics.

Robots and Androids. "Military Robots." Retrieved August 7,

2018. http://www.robots-and-androids.com/military -robots.html.

Rosenbaum, Steven. "Humans vs. Robots—Who's on Top?" *Forbes*, November 26, 2012. https://www .forbes.com/sites/stevenrosenbaum/2012/11/26 /humans-vs-robots-whos-on-top/#2bd32b8867bd.

Study.com. "Robotics Training Programs and Requirements." Retrieved August 8, 2018. https://study.com/robotics _training.html.

Tagaban, Juvanell. "Different Types of Industrial Robots and Applications." Web2u43, January 3, 2018. https:// web2u43.com/industrial-robots-types-applications.

Tarpey, Matthew. "Mobile Job Searching Gets Augmented." CareerBuilder, September 11, 2018. https://www .careerbuilder.com/advice/mobile-app-job-search.

US Department of Labor, Bureau of Labor Statistics. *Occupational Outlook Handbook*. "Mechanical Engineers." Updated April 13, 2018. https://www.bls.gov/ooh /architecture-and-engineering/mechanical-engineers .htm.

INDEX

A

Alexa, 20
artificial intelligence (AI), 32, 33,
    34–36, 44, 46, 51
Asimov, Isaac, 6
  Three Laws of Robotics, 41
autism, 26, 33

B

BeatBots, 33
BigDog, 42, 44
Bo, 23
BOX (RobotLAB), 23
Bureau of Labor Statistics, 55

C

Cantlie, Charity, 5
CareerBuilder, 60
Carnegie Mellon University, 12
  Robotics Club (Roboclub),
    12–14
Castilleja School, 12
CHARISMA Research Lab, 50
computational thinking, 17, 19
  example problem, 20–22
  three-step process in, 19–20
cover letters, 60, 62
Cubelets, 6
Curiosity, 42

D

da Vinci Surgical System, 32–33
Davis, Michelle, 4
drones, 42
Dyson 360 Eye, 29–30

E

Edison, Thomas, 13
EZ-Robot, 23

F

FANUC America, 55
FIRST LEGO League
    Competition, 12
FIRST Robotics Competition, 12
Fleming, Laura, 14–16

G

Gibson, Tyler, 25–26
Gleneagles (elementary school),
    4–6
Goliath, 40

H

hackerspace, 9
Howard, Ayanna, 22

K

Keepon, 33
Knight, Heather, 50
Kohn, Marty, 35–36

L

Lau, Tessa, 29
Linkbots, 24
Loup Ventures. 38

M

makerspace, 52
    defined, 4
    finding, 7, 9–10
    goals of, 14–16
    at home, 13
    vs. hackerspace, 9
Makerspaces.com, 9
Marathon Targets, 44
Max Planck Institute, 33
mechanical engineers, 55–56
Michalowski, Marek, 33
microbots, 33–34
Miller, Foster, 44
Miller, Liz, 58–59
Modular Robotics (website), 13
MQ-1 Predator, 42
Munster, Gene, 32

N

NAO, 23, 26
New Media Consortium and the

Consortium for School
Networking, 6

O

Opportunity, 42
Osladil, Tony, 24
Owen-Hill, Alex, 51

P

Pi-Bot, 23

R

résumés, 62–63
Robot for Interactive Body
    Assistance (RIBA), 32
robotics
    advanced degrees, 54
    applying for, 60, 62–63
    careers in, 47, 49
    certification, 54–55
    college degrees, 52–54
    high school courses, 49, 51–52
    interviewing for, 63–65
    salary, 55
    searching for jobs in, 57–60
    skills needed, 49
    working in field, 65–66
robotics engineers, 55–56, 59
RobotLAB, 23
robots
    in the classroom, 22–24,
        25–26
    collaborative, 40

home, 27, 29–32
industrial, 37–38, 40
on Mars, 22, 42–43
medical, 32–36
military, 40–42, 44–46
Robots and Androids (website), 41
Roomba, 27, 29

S

Savioke, 29
science, technology, engineering,
    and math (STEM), 4
science, technology, engineering,
    arts, and math (STEAM), 4
Shafer, Nancy, 24
Sierra College Robotics Club, 24
Sojourner, 22
Spencer, John, 10–12
Spheros, 5
Storybird, 5–6

T

TALON, 44
Teletanks, 40–41
Thailand cave rescue, 44–45
TUG robot, 32

U

UNISONO project, 43
unmanned aerial vehicles
    (UAVs), 42
unmanned ground vehicles
    (UGVs), 42, 44

unmanned underwater vehicles
    (UUVs), 44

V

Veebot, 32
Vesta, 30–31
VEX Robotic Station, 5
VGo, 26

W

Watson, 34–36
Wilson, Cari, 5
Wing, Jeannette, 19, 20

X

Xenex robot, 32

Y

Yana, 23

Z

Zenbo, 30

ABOUT THE AUTHOR

Carol Hand has a PhD in zoology with a specialization in ecology and environmental problems. She has taught at colleges, worked for standardized testing companies, developed multimedia science and technology curricula, and written numerous books for young people, most on science and technology. Her technology titles include *Filter Bubbles and You*, *Getting Paid to Produce Videos*, *Hi-Tech Criminal Justice*, *Tech Careers for Girls*, and *How the Internet Changed History*.

PHOTO CREDITS

Cover (top), p. 1 troyek/E+/Getty Images; cover (bottom) Monty Rakusen/Cultura/Getty Images; p. 5 © iStockphoto.com/Steve Debenport; p. 8 Education Images/UIG/Getty Images; pp. 10–11 Courtesy Castilleja School; pp. 14–15 gipi23/E+/Getty Images; pp. 18–19 © iStockphoto.com/asiseeit; pp. 20–21 Steve Rogers Photography/Getty Images; p. 25 © AP Images; p. 28 Douglas McFadd/Getty Images; p. 31 Juan Ci/Shutterstock.com; pp. 34–35 Ben Hider/Getty Images; p. 38 Surasak_Photo/Shutterstock.com; p. 41 Interim Archives/Archive Photos/Getty Images; p. 43 NASA/JPL-Caltech; p. 45 Lillian Suwanrumpha/AFP/Getty Images; p. 48 picture alliance/Getty Images; p. 49 © iStockphoto.com/svetikd; pp. 52–53 Troy House/Corbis NX/Getty Images; p. 58 Dragon Images/Shutterstock.com; p. 61 Andrey_Popov/Shutterstock.com; p. 63 mavo/Shutterstock.com; interior pages background (drone illustration) brovkin/Shutterstock.com; cover graphic Pobytov/DigitalVision Vectors/Getty Images; p. 4 illustration Bloomicon/Shutterstock.com.

Design: Michael Moy; Editor: Bethany Bryan; Photo Researcher: Nicole DiMella